IMPROVISATION STEP BY STEP

IMPROVISING CLASSICAL MUSIC ON PIANO

by Misha V. Stefanuk

This book teaches the improvisation of classical music through a step by step method. By practicing simple tasks the pianist escapes the psychological pressure of performing on the spot and develops the ease and freedom of improvising in classical styles. This book also includes 7 variations on a theme by Beethoven illustrating the improvisational concept and technique.

www.melbay.com/99657BCDEB

Audio Contents

1 2 3 4 5 6 7 8 9 0

Visit us on the Web at www.melbay.com — E-mail us at email@melbay.com

Table of Contents

Part I: Alphabet of Improvisation

Part II. Language of Improvisation

Part III. Styles

Part I: Alphabet of Improvisation

Chapter One

Introduction

This chapter introduces the concept of ornamentation and provides examples of common ornaments.

Many people do not feel comfortable when asked to do something completely new. Starting to improvise is one of the steps that many musicians never take. On the other hand, most musicians who do improvise can not imagine how it could seem difficult to so many others. Once a pianist starts improvising, there is no way back, but it might be a difficult step for many musicians. This book will help to make this step less intimidating.

Psychologically, it is hard to overcome the fear of the very first step. This book makes it much easier through a step by step method. A pianist is asked to do simple things that increase in difficulty gradually, eliminating the necessity to create a great piece of music on the spot without experience and necessary knowledge. Musicians are often embarrassed to improvise, so instead they are asked to perform very simple tasks and then gradually make improvising more complex.

We will use chord charts like those used in popular music and start from creating a simple piece in a quasi-Romantic style. This is our first chart:

C	Am	F	G7
C	Am	Dm	Dm
F	G7	C	Am
Dm	G7	C	C

To create a piece of music using this progression, one must become familiar with the chords from which it is made. (Notice: all examples in this book should be both played as written and then improvised.)

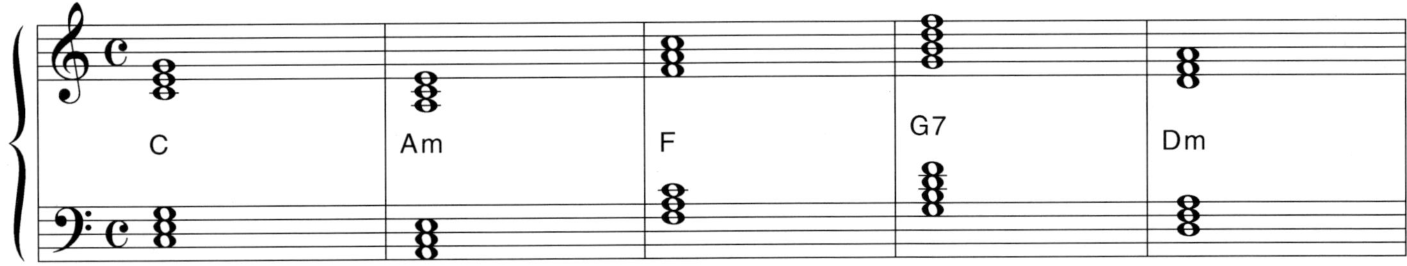

One should take the time to slowly and efficiently figure out the notes these chords consist of and write them down. Then the chords should be practiced until they become very easy to find.

Next one should become familiar with the chord structure and, if needed, write it down and practice:

COMPACT disc DIGITAL AUDIO TRACK 1

C | Am | F | G7

5

C | Am | Dm | Dm

9

F | G7 | C | Am

13

Dm | G7 | C | C

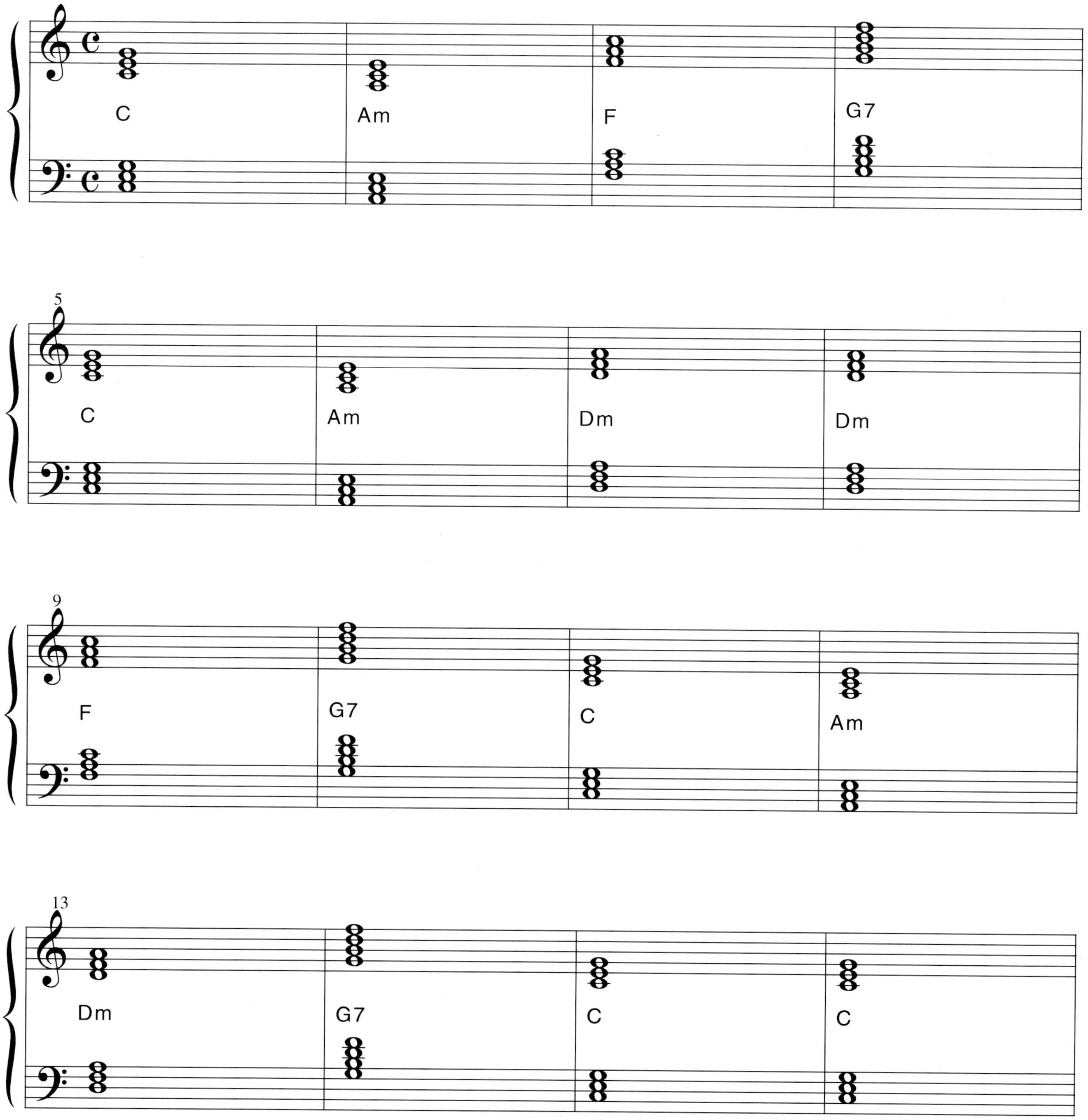

To further advance the knowledge of the progression, play the possible chord inversions as well:

Next, to start making a piece of music out of the chord progression, the left hand part should be developed. Use a very simple I-V-I figure for every chord:

After some practice, this becomes an easy task. The next step is to start the improvisation in the right hand. Start with chord tones on all four beats, with the left hand playing the earlier developed bass line:

The next step in improving our improvisation is using chord inversions to create a smoother melodic line and to eliminate big interval jumps at the beginning of each bar:

Playing all quarters and a left hand in time is not very hard, but it will take some practice before it becomes very smooth and easy. Technically, this can already be called improvisation.

Now it is time to make it sound more musical. Slightly modify the rhythm for the right hand by changing the two first quarter notes of each measure to dotted quarters and an eighth. Also cut out the eighth quarter note in each group:

Now we can further modify the rhythm by adding two eighth notes to every other group of two measures:

The next step in improving the improvisational technique is adding a very simple leading tone on the last eighth note of every other bar. It should be a note a half tone away from the first note of the next bar:

Notice that in bar 9 we had to use the leading note on the opposite side of the coming chord tone.

Adding a little finishing touch- let's make sure that the last note of the 8th and 16th bars in the right hand is a tonic. Let's also change the rhythm in the very last bar to a quarter note followed by two eighth notes and another quarter. This will give the ending a final cadence feel:

The steps above were not very difficult or scary, and we ended up with a very nice sounding piece of improvised music. The step by step method rewards pianists with a quick result and a sense of accomplishment that will keep them interested in playing more and more.

Chapter Two

Arpeggios and Rhythm Formulas

This chapter introduces the concept of ornamentation and provides examples of common ornaments.

To further improve the musical quality of our example, we will work a little more on the right hand part. First we will play eighth note arpeggios based on the chord structure all the way through the piece:

Even though the previous example was very easy to perform, there was too much jumping in the right hand part. If we were to use smoother voice leading, it would become less predictable and sound much better:

Next, we develop our eighth note arpeggios with appropriate voice leading into one another. We also freely alternate the direction of the improvised line. To improvise in this way, one would read the previous chart and end up playing this:

Now, let's work a little on the rhythm. Playing all eighth notes becomes monotonous; it sounds like somebody who keeps talking very fast for a very long time. Let's imagine that this talking person finds it necessary to breathe once in a while- let's say every 3 to 7 notes. Play the previous example pausing from time to time:

This sounds more like human speech, and it makes more sense.

Let's go back and also use the idea of preset rhythmic formulas. We will use the dotted quarter-eighth-quarter- two eighths figure:

Now we will alternate the preset rhythmic formula that we have just developed with the eighth note arpeggios and use the idea of taking a breath once in a while:

The last example can be varied by simply changing the order of the preset rhythmic formula and arpeggios. Let's say that bars 1,4,6 and 7 use a preset rhythmic formula, and bars 2,3,5 and 8 use eighth note arpeggios:

When improvising, it is very helpful to alternate these two ideas freely without having to remember which formula comes next. After a little practicing, it becomes easy and comfortable.

Chapter Three

Leading Notes

This chapter introduces the concept of ornamentation and provides examples of common ornaments.

Earlier we introduced the idea of the leading note as the last note leading into the next bar. The following example uses leading notes going into first and third beat of each bar:

Changing the direction in which the leading tone approaches the chord tone gives us two possibilities instead of just one. Also, sometimes both leading notes can be used in succession:

We will now play the combination of eighth note arpeggios with leading notes before each bar. It is important to spend time with each one of these easy steps because combining them together requires a certain level of familiarity and ease in using them:

Now we can add another leading note before the third beat in each bar:

In order to make the music less predictable and therefore more interesting to listen to, let's use leading notes randomly combined with arpeggios:

The next step to improve our improvisation technique is adding one more leading note to the preexisting leading note. We will simply have two notes that are a half step apart leading into the following chord note. We will start by playing these combinations leading into each measure:

Let's now combine the eighth note arpeggios, leading notes in both directions and double leading notes freely in one piece. It would be very helpful to start by playing this exercise very slowly, so that there is enough time to think and make choices:

Chapter Four

Chord Tone Approaches

This chapter introduces the system of chord tone approaches and demostrates incorporating them into the musical material.

Another way of categorizing non-chord tones is using the system of chord tone approaches or CTA's. The simplest way of approaching the chord note is using notes a half step up or down from the chord tone in sequence. This gives us two possible approaches:

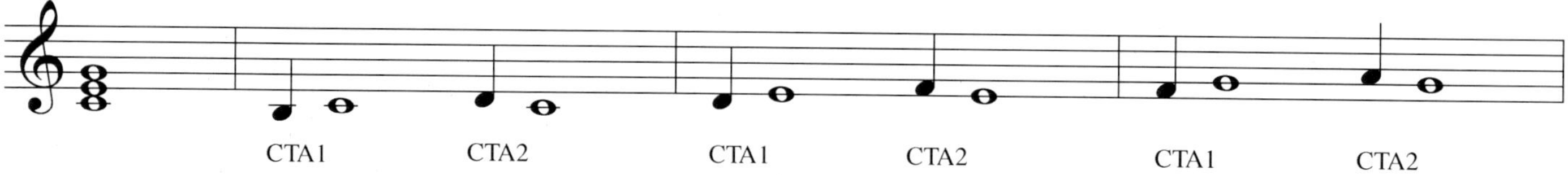

The next two chord tone approaches are much like double leading notes:

The last group of chord tone approaches uses notes on both sides of the chord tone. The important difference between these and leading notes is that these CTA's do not necessarily have to be half step away. The following examples illustrates both kinds of CTA's - a half step and a whole step from the chord note:

Here is a chart of all chord tone approaches (CTA's) by numbers with all interval possibilities:

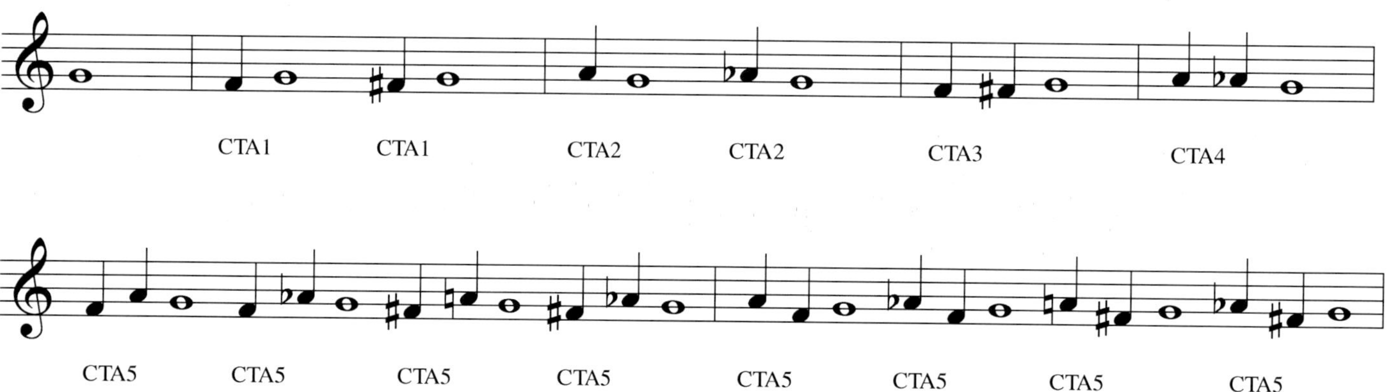

Let's use these chord tone approaches leading into the first and third beat of each bar of our original chord progression:

Now it is time to incorporate CTA's into a musical piece by combining them with eighth note arpeggios:

Combining this technique with the use of a rhythm formula of a dotted quarter-eighth-quarter-two eighths:

Chapter Five

Scales

This chapter introduces scales and discusses how to incorporate them into previously learned material.

More musical material can be developed by using different scales. Each chord calls for the use of a specific scale to be played with it. A Major chord calls for a Major or Lydian scale:

CMaj Major Lydian

A Dominant, or 7th chord, calls for the use of the mixolydian or whole-tone scale:

C7 Mixolydian Whole-Tone

A minor chord calls for the use of a minor or dorian scale:

Cmin Minor Dorian

A diminished chord calls for a locrian or half-whole diminished scale:

Cdim Locrian Half-Whole-Diminished

An augmented chord calls for an augmented or whole-tone scale:

CAug Augmented Whole-Tone

Let's use the appropriate scales moving in eighth notes in our piece:

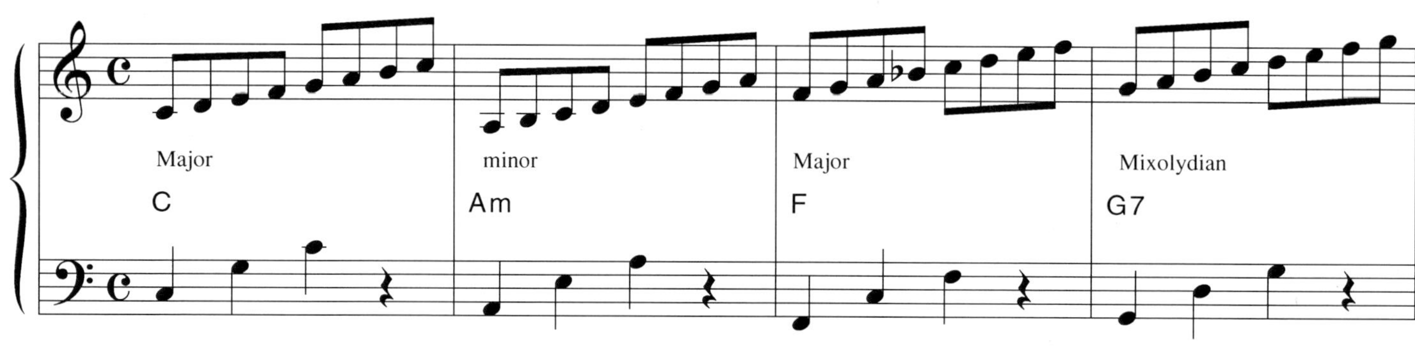

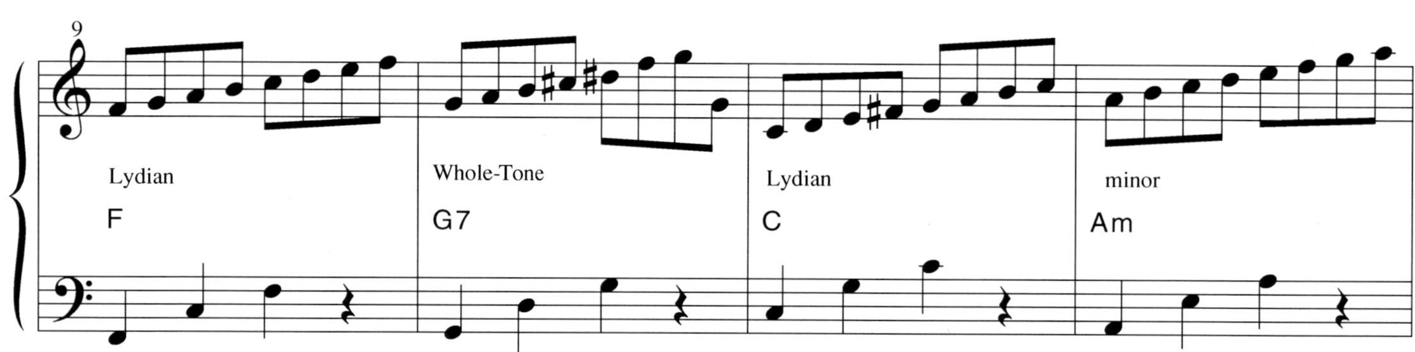

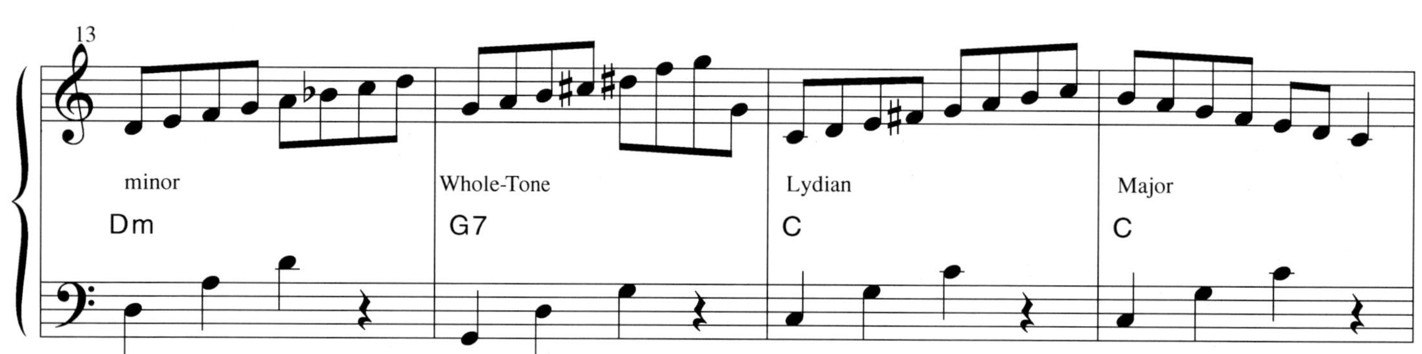

To make the melodic line smoother, every scale should start somewhere close to the last note of the previous scale:

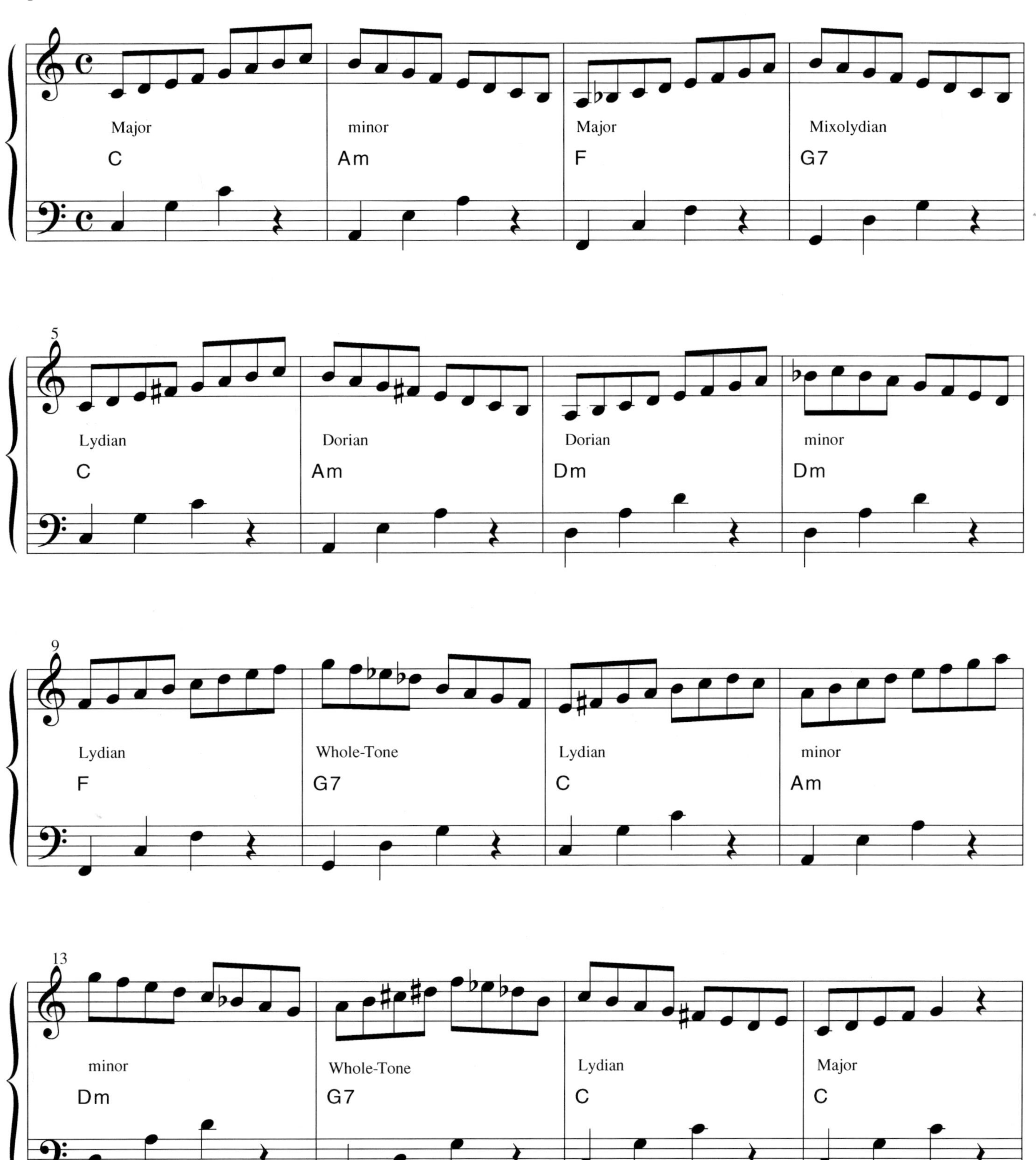

It is very effective to alternate scales with arpeggios:

Just as we did with eighth notes arpeggios earlier, we need to make these lines breathe by adding rests ever so often:

For practicing, it is very helpful to use lines going up for one bar and then down for one bar:

To gain more control over the direction of the melodic line, a line of two bars up and two bars down should be practiced:

Combining direction control and breathing creates a wonderful line:

Using scales greatly enhances the melody, and it should be practiced until it becomes a very natural way of improvising.

Chapter Six

Combining Scales, Arpeggios, Rhythmic Formulas and Chord Tone Approaches

This chapter combines all previously learned concepts.

To develop the ease of combining the scales with arpeggios we will start with alternating them each bar:

The next example alternates arpeggios and scales every two measures:

The formula for the next exercise is one bar arpeggio up, two bars of scales down:

After all of previous exercises become easy to perform, we should use free combinations of arpeggios and scales without a preset formula:

The next step is combining scales and arpeggios with leading notes and chord tone approaches. Let's start with a formula that uses CTA's leading into beat 1 of each measure, leaving the rest of the space for arpeggios and scales:

We must remember to add rests from time to time to allow the musical material to breathe:

Next we need to incorporate the preset rhythmic formulas into improvisation. Let's use the following rhythmic formula:

The last exercise in this chapter combines scales, arpeggios and preset rhythmic formulas freely:

Combining scales, arpeggios, preset rhythmic formulas and chord tone approaches gives us plenty of choices to build endless improvisations.

Chapter Seven

Creating Original Melodic Patterns

This chapter discusses the creating of original melodic patterns
and incorporating them into a musical piece.

In this chapter we will talk about creating our own preset melodic patterns. After a little experimenting with improvisation we find out that our improvised lines repeat some recognizable fragments. Unconsciously, the improviser remembers some more successful lines and they become a part of one's personal language.
The most common use for preset melodic lines would be in measures with a cadenza character- bars 4, 8, 12 and 16. It might be helpful to tape your own improvisation, listen for more successful fragments and write them down in order to reproduce them again. The following example shows our harmonic structure with a preconceived cadenza melodies:

This is how the completed improvisation would sound:

The use of the preconceived fragments also helps make the improvisation sound more professional. It serves the function of a frame around a painting. After writing down and memorizing about 4 to 6 fragments for a cadenza, one should start incorporating them into an improvised piece of music.

Let's start by composing two cadenzas for bars 8 and 12, writing them into the next chart and improvising all the rest using scales and arpeggios:

The other common type of preconceived fragments is just a melodic phrase that fits one chord change and is practiced and memorized in all twelve keys. This is an example of such a fragment and the use of it:

Practice improvising using one, then two, and then both of the following fragments:

Write in your own fragments and practice improvising including them into musical material:

Chapter Eight

The Relationship of Rhythm and Harmony

This chapter explains the use of chord and non-chord tones on strong and weak beats of the bar.

A scale used with a particular chord contains chord tones as well as non-chord notes. In the following example chord tones are displayed as whole notes, and non-chord tones are displayed as quarter notes:

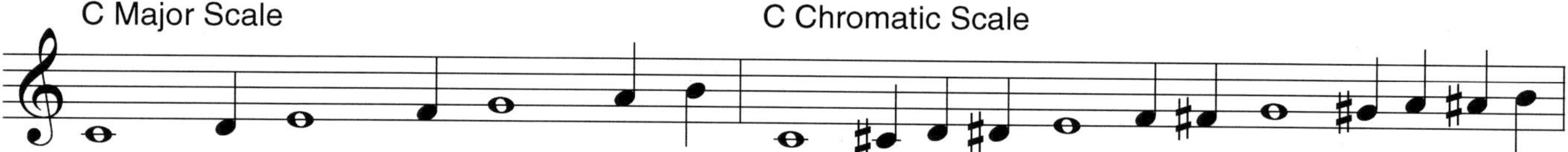

A 4/4 bar has two strong beats- 1 and 3, and two weak beats- 2 and 4. Usually, the improvised line uses chord tones on strong beats rather than non-chord tones:

Sometimes it is more effective to pause the movement for a couple of eighth notes in order to have the chord tone on the strong beat:

Another way of resulting in a chord note on the strong beat is to jump into it rather than continuing scalar movement:

Sometimes chord tones occur on all four beats in order to emphasize the presence of the chord:

Try to improvise scales using chord tones on beats 1 and 3:

Another way of accenting chord tones is to start and end phrases on chord tones.

C Major Scale

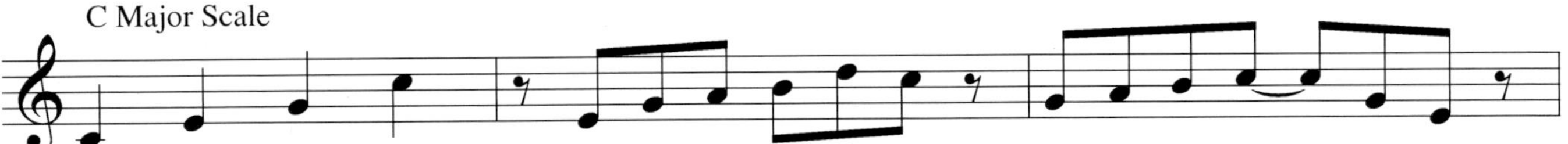

Now, try to use these techniques with our original chord progression.
The right hand part contains chord tones:

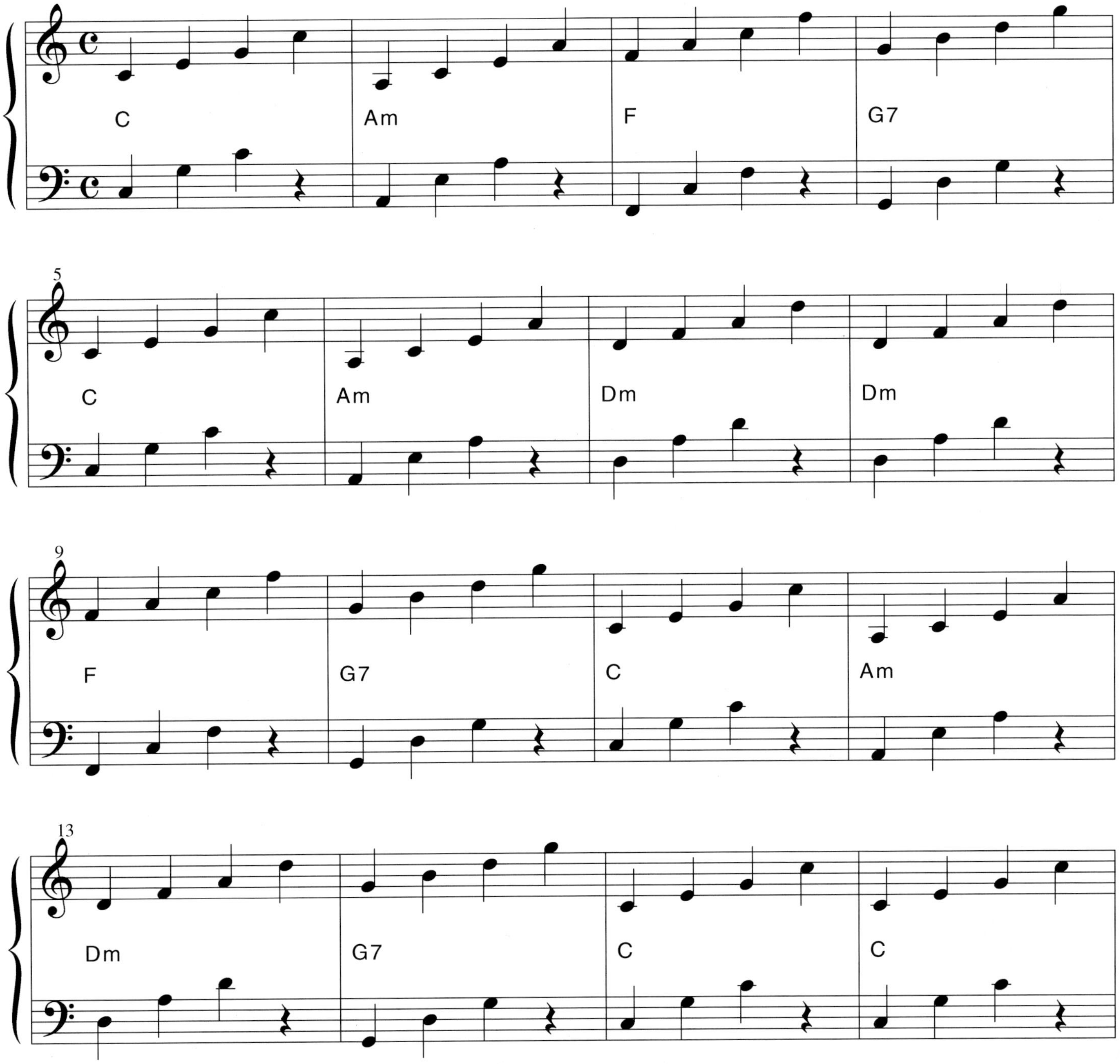
C
Am
F
G7
5
C
Am
Dm
Dm
9
F
G7
C
Am
13
Dm
G7
C
C

Accenting chord tones by using them on strong beats and by using them to start and end the phrase increases the feeling of tonality.

Chapter Nine

A Traditional Approach to Non-Chord Tones

This chapter introduces the traditional terminology and approach to non-chord tones.

As we established earlier, the way we use chord tones is different from the way we use non-chord tones. The reason for this is the differing character of their sound. Chord tones sound very stable, while non-chord tones sound less stable and tend to move into a neighboring chord tone. The instability of non-chord tones is called tension, and its movement to the chord tone is called resolution:

Notes placed a half step from the chord tone create stronger tension for resolution than notes that are farther away:

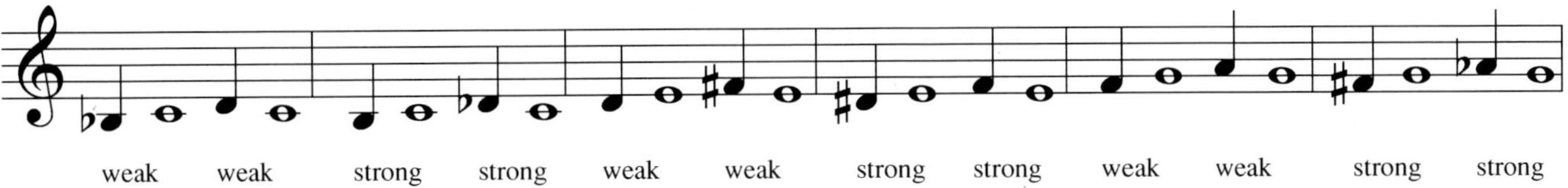

The following example shows the use of non-chord tones with a strong tension to accent the chord tones on the strong beats:

In traditional theory non-chord tones are divided into four groups: passing tones, anticipations, suspensions and neighbor notes. A passing tone is a note or a group of notes placed between two chord tones:

An anticipation is a chord tone that is played slightly before the strong beat or a chord change:

A suspension is a chord tone that is played longer than the chord to which it belongs so that it becomes a non-chord tone to the new chord:

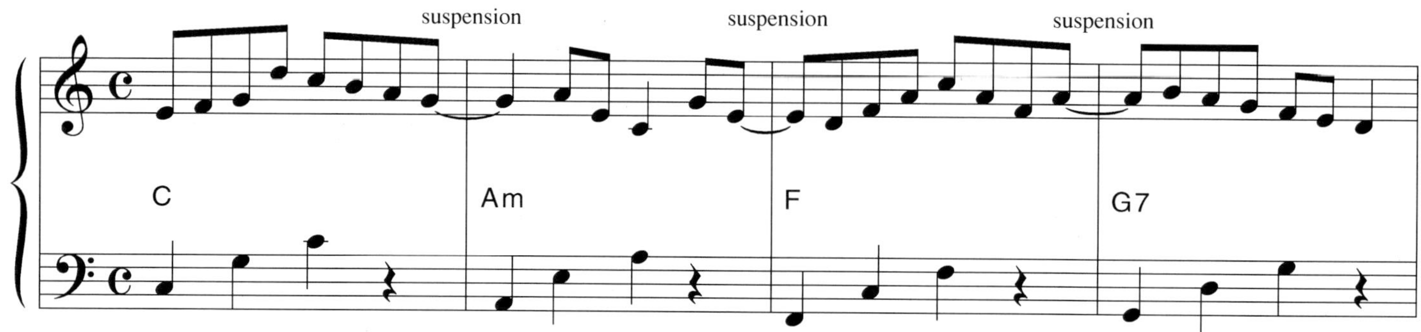

The last kind of non-chord tone is the neighbor note- a note or group of notes around the chord tone:

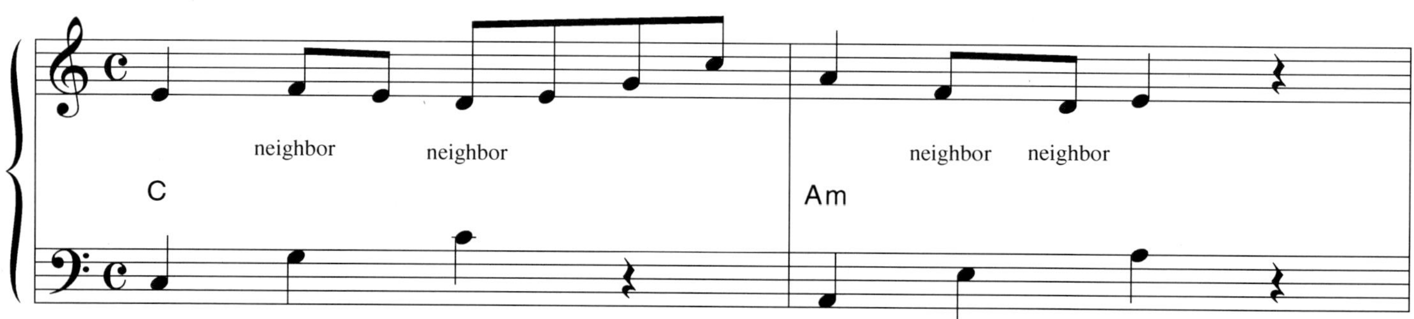

Use all 4 kinds of non-chord tones around the chord tones on beats 1 and 3:

Chapter Ten

Motivic Development

This chapter introduces motives and motivic development.

A motive is a group of 3 or more notes that has a recognizable character. The following example has four motives from well-known musical pieces:

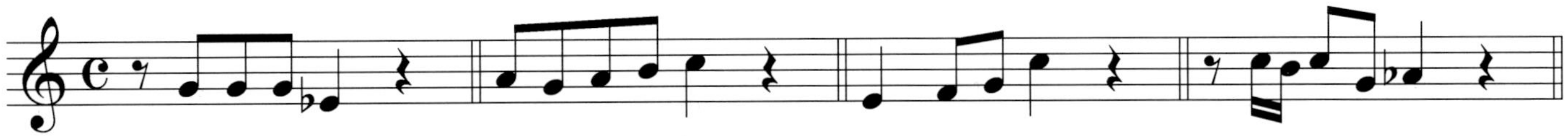

Motives are usually not longer than five to seven notes. A very important defining characteristic is the direction of the motive:

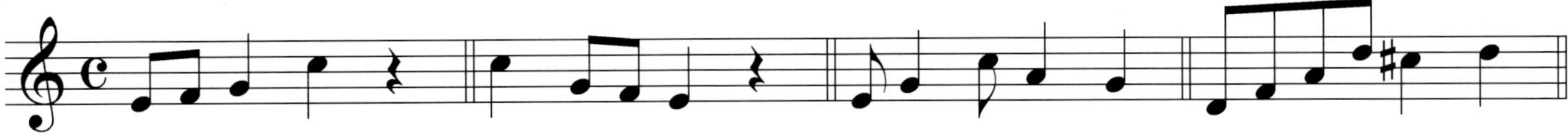

Another important factor is the rhythmic construction of the motive:

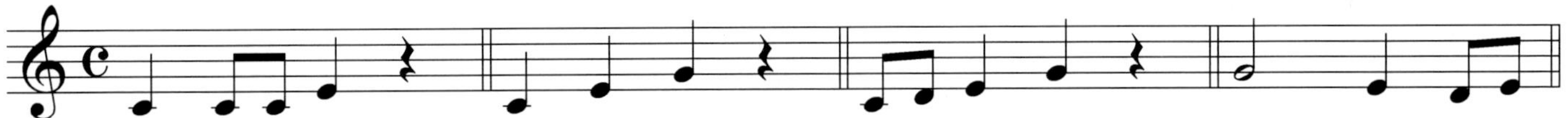

A motive can be constructed of chord tones only, or use a combination of chord tones and non-chord tones

Combining these factors, we can create motives that feel very solid and stable or very unstable:

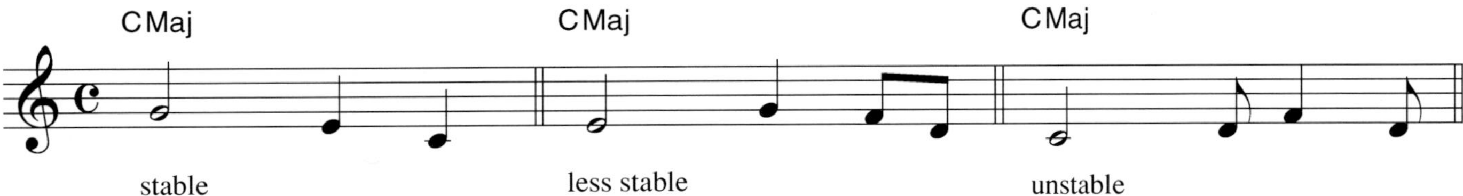

Next we will discuss motivic development. After analyzing a motive, we determine its typical characteristics- the notes it consists of, the direction, the rhythm and the level of its stability. For example the following motive consists of chord tones only, has a downward contour, begins on the weak beat and ends on the strong beat, and is very stable:

There are four different ways to state the motive: repetition, retrograde, inversion and retrograde inversion. Retrograde is stating the motive backwards:

Inversion is flipping the motive upside down while keeping the distances between the notes the same:

Retrograde inversion is a combination of a retrograde and inversion:

While improvising, it is important to make statements of the motive recognizable rather than trying to make them exact:

Improvise using the 4 kinds of motive repetition with these motives as material for repetition:

In improvisation it is very useful to find one or two main characteristic motives and use them occasionally in improvised lines.

Compose your own motives, and use them freely with improvised lines:

A very effective way to create musical interest is using diminution and augmentation. Diminution of the rhythm is shortening the duration of notes:

Augmentation is the opposite process- it is elongating the duration of notes:

Augmentation is often used to make the motive sound more substantial and impressive.

Use the following motives and their augmented or diminished forms:

One of the most common ways of developing a motive is changing the intervals it consists of:

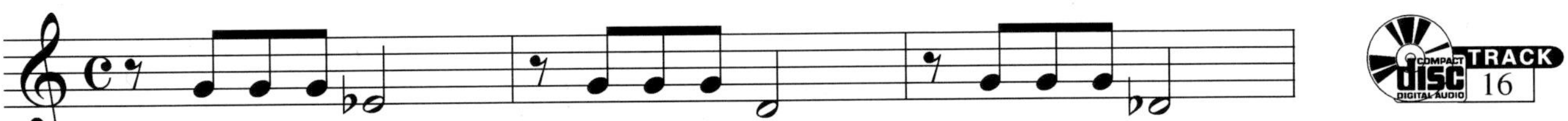

The changing of the intervals of a motive can vary from very subtle to very radical, but the motive should stay recognizable:

Often the motive is very strong rhythmically. Even after changing all of the intervals it consists of, the motive is still recognizable:

However, there are motives which lack strong rhythmical personality. In this case, retaining the original intervals becomes more important:

Generally, motivic development helps to keep music well organized. Combined with the use of arpeggios, scales, rhythmic formulas and non-chord tones, motivic development creates many possibilities for improvisation.

Use the following motives and their forms with different intervals for your improvisation:

Using good motivic development is a sign of a highly intellectual musician. It makes the form more solid and unifies the musical material.

Part II: Language of Improvisation

Chapter Eleven

Melody

This chapter discusses the development of melody out of motives.

The combination of motives creates a melody- a line with a distinct and finished character:

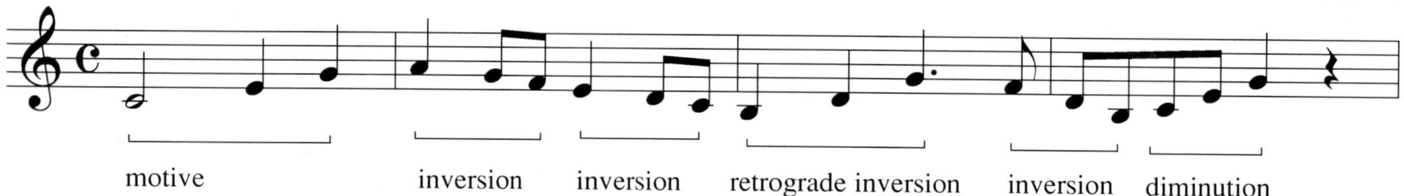

Melody is a tune that becomes material for improvisation. Quite often melody is eight or sixteen bars long. For example, this is an eight bar melody from Mozart's Sonata in Bb Major

To develop the melody, we need to use motivic development. After determining the main characteristics of the motives in the melody we can further develop them:

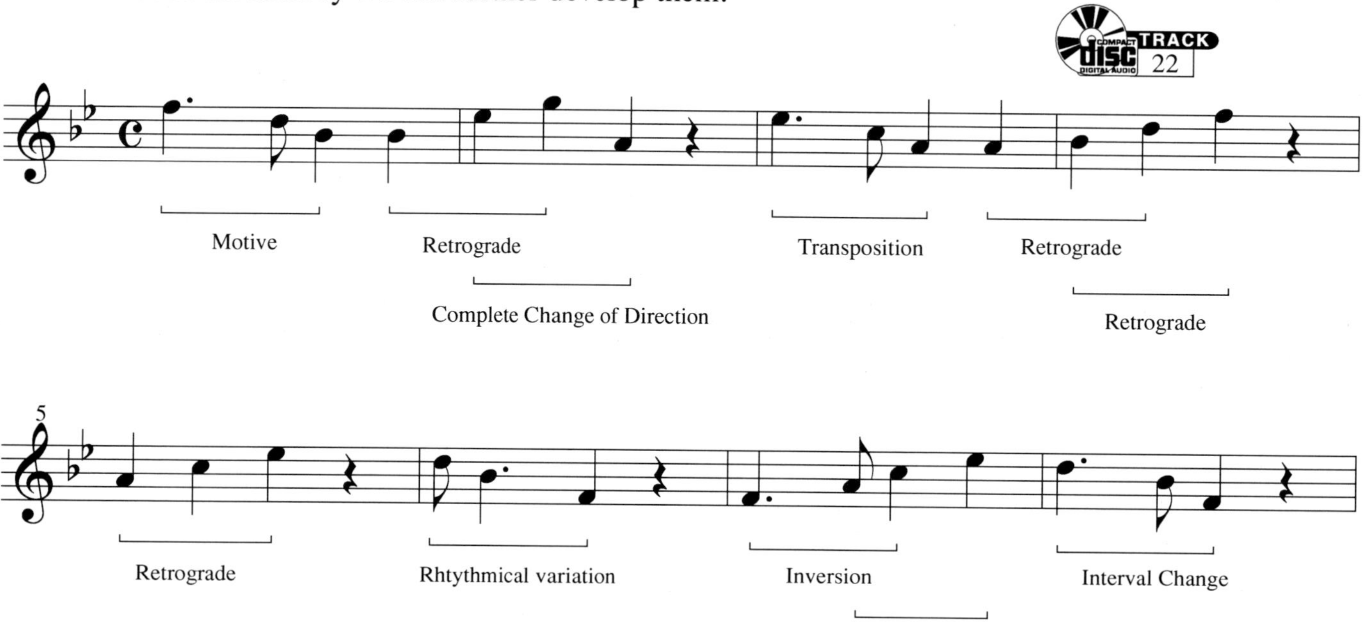

A melody should have a very distinct closing. It often resolves into the tonic chord (I, or C Major chord in the key of C Major) on the first beat of the last bar or into the Dominant (V, or G Major or G7th chord in C Major) in the last bar:

The opening motive can be brought back in its original form at the end of the melody, or it may be slightly modified in order to achieve a better resolution:

When improvising using a given opening motive, it is helpful to practice its four variations first:

TRACK 23

Motive
Inversion
Retrograde
Retrograde Inversion

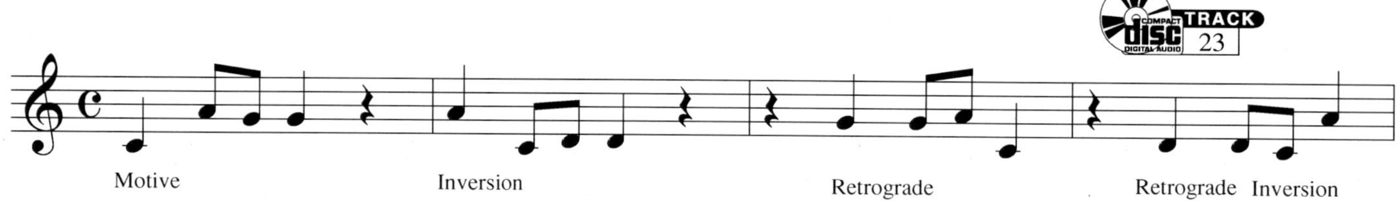

Then we need to use one of these variations in bars 8, 12 and 16:

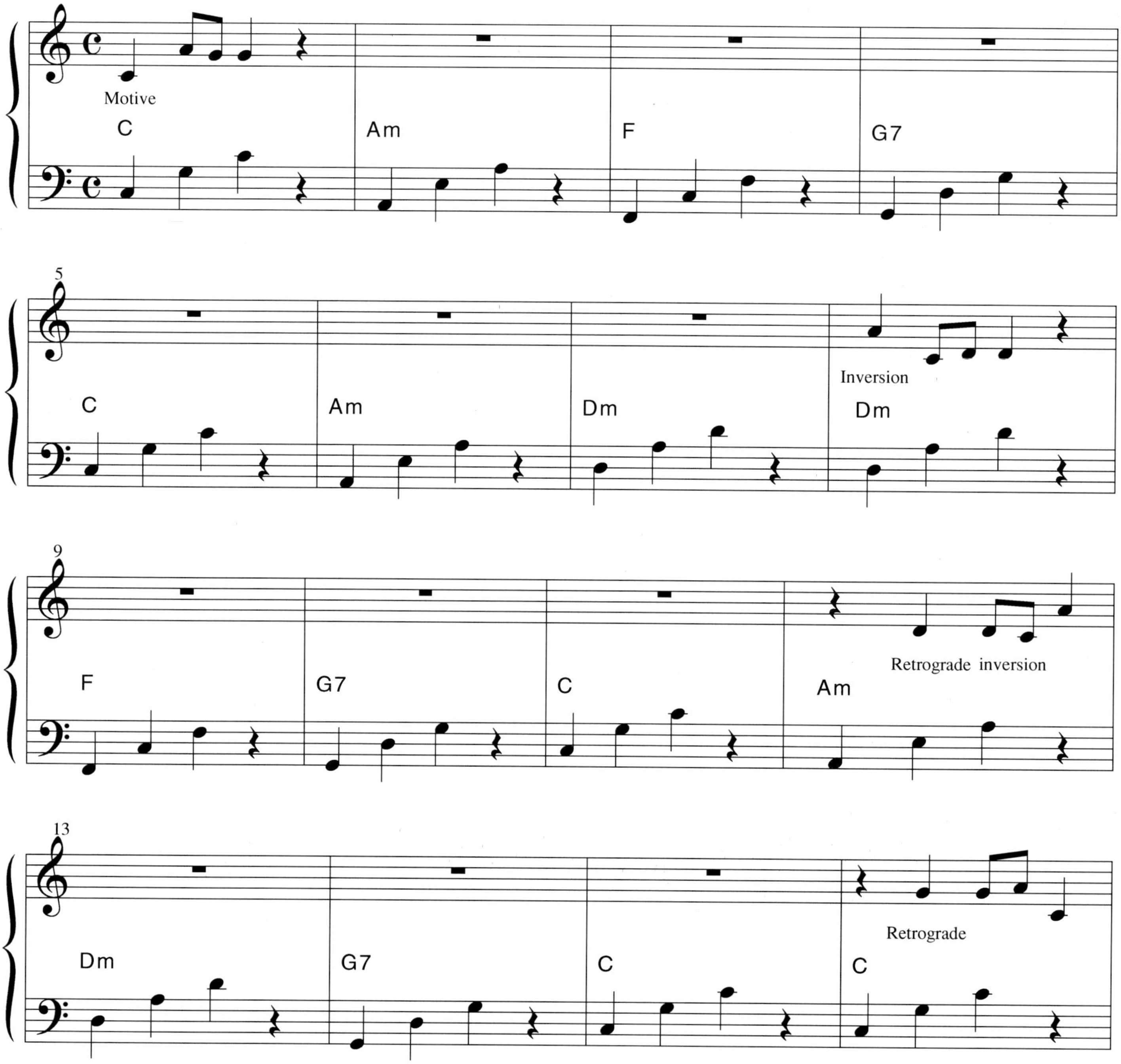

Motive
C
Am
F
G7
5
C
Am
Dm
Inversion
Dm
9
F
G7
C
Retrograde inversion
Am
13
Dm
G7
C
Retrograde
C

In the following example, use variations of the opening motive in bar 16 and also four times somewhere in the middle of the improvised lines:

Chapter Twelve

The Relationship Between Improvisation and Original Melody

This chapter discusses the relationship of the improvised material with the original melody.

Usually a melody chosen for improvisation has a strong tonal and rhythmic character. There are many ways that the melody can be used in the improvisation. The simplest way to use the melody is to repeat it with some minor changes. The following example has the first 4 bars of the original melody and the first 4 bars of the first variation. The pianist can use all kinds of non-chord tones for added notes:

Play the following 8 bar melody adding various non-chord tones: passing tones, anticipations, suspensions and neighbor notes:

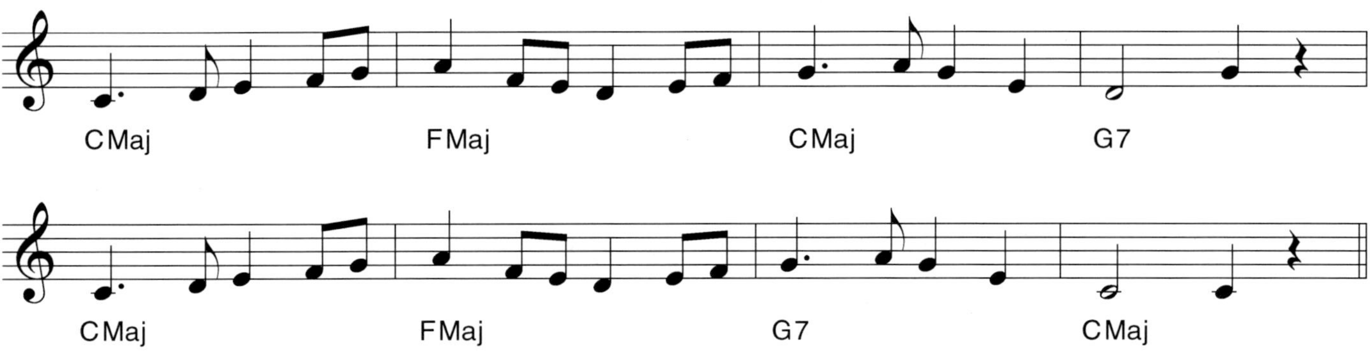

The long notes and rests in the melody can be replaced with scales:

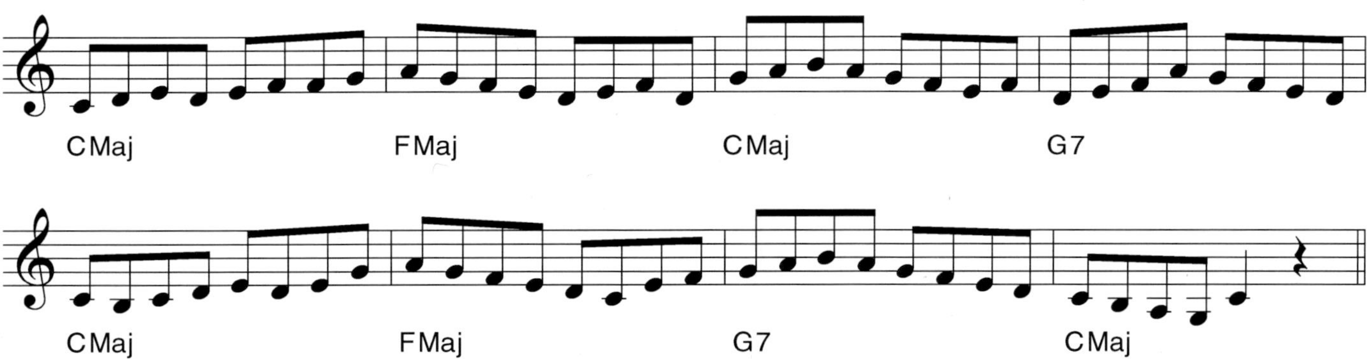

It also can be done with arpeggios:

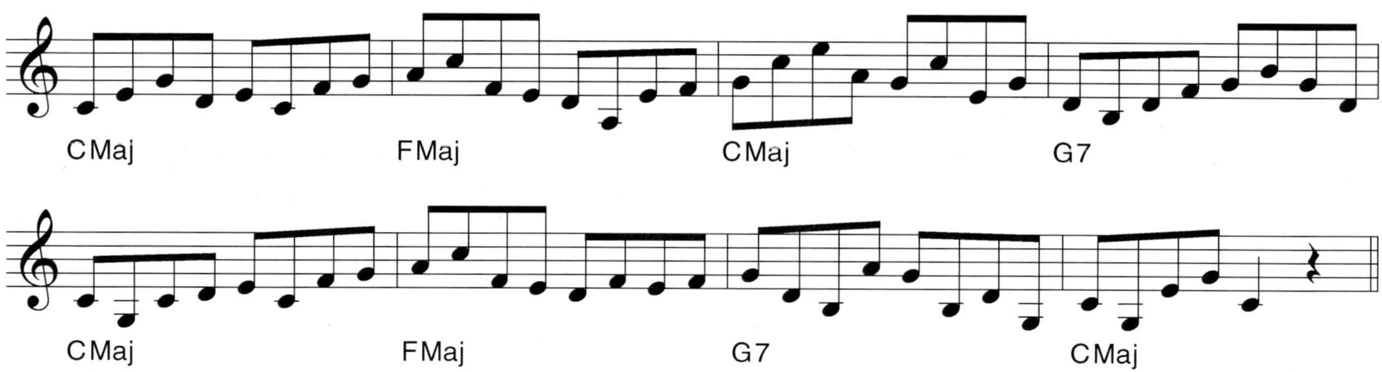

Sometimes a significant part of the melody can be replaced by improvisation, and then a return to the original melodic material would be very successful:

Sometimes the material of the original melody can be misplaced in the harmonic structure:

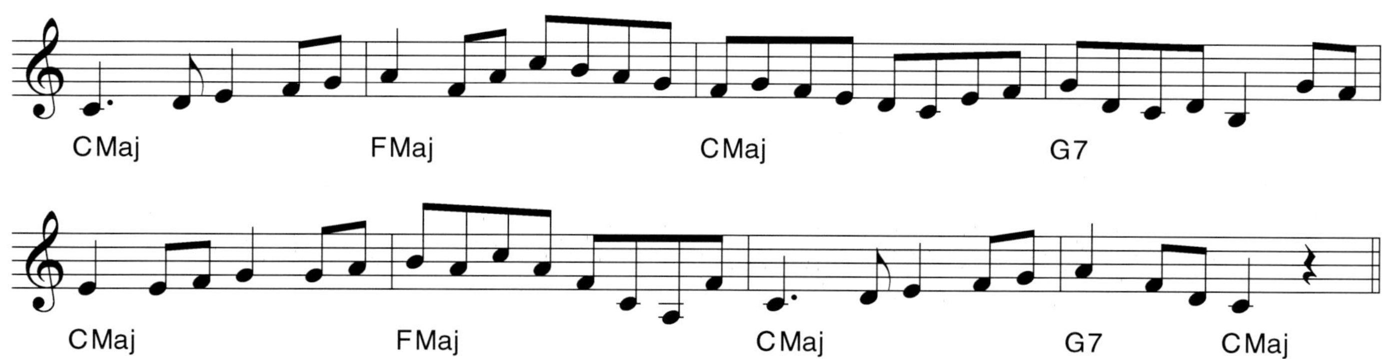

The use of retrograde and inversion can be very helpful and provide more choices:

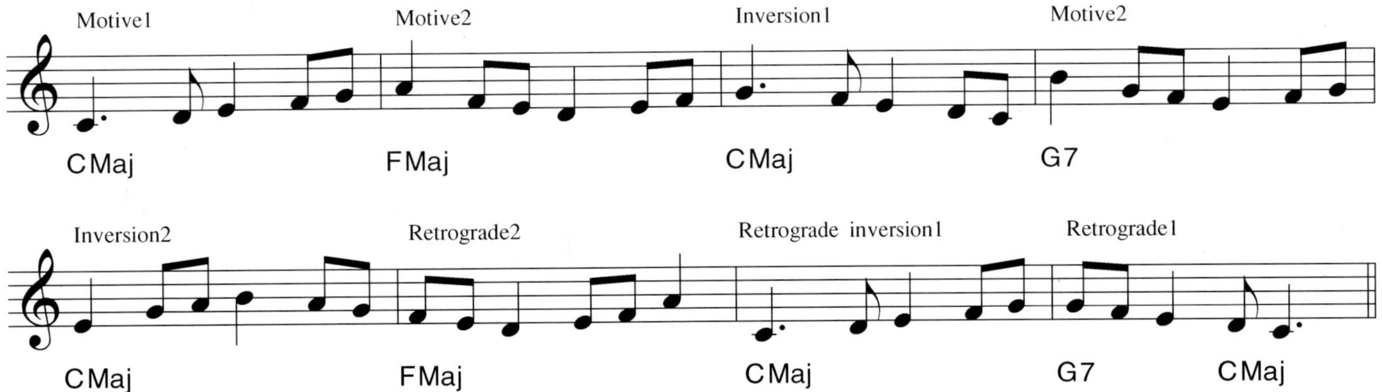

Use motives of the original melody in retrograde or inversion when indicated, and fill the rest with scales and arpeggios:

Motive1 Motive2

C Am F G7

5

Motive2 Retrograde1

C Am Dm Dm

9

Retrograde2 Inversion1

F G7 C Am

13

Motive1 Retrograde2

Dm G7 C C

Chapter Thirteen

Ornamentation

This chapter introduces the concept of ornamentation and provides examples of common ornaments.

Ornamenting is creating decorations around the melody notes that enhance the melody and make it more interesting. There are many ornaments in classical music widely used to vary the presentation of the melody. A mordent is one of the most common ornaments:

Often in baroque music the mordent will be written down as a symbol only. The other form of mordent reverses the direction:

A trill is another widely used ornament:

Ideally, a trill is very fast, and there is often a mordent that can be used at the end of a trill:

Another type of ornament is a very fast run, usually a scale or an arpeggio:

The following example should be played as written and then with ornaments:

The amount of ornamentation used depends upon personal preference. Sometimes the use of very few ornaments will vary original character of the tune significantly:

At other times there may be so many ornaments used that the melody itself becomes unrecognizable:

We know the term augmentation as the process of elongating the actual melody. This term can also refer to the use of longer rhythmical durations with no reference to pitch or melody. The term diminution can likewise refer to the use of smaller rhythmical durations in musical material, also with no reference to pitch. In the following example the augmented version moves in half notes, and the diminished in eight notes, contrasting to the quarter movement of the original melody:

Typically, if the melody uses mostly quarter notes with the first variation consisting mostly of eighth notes and the second consisting of mostly eighth triplets and sixteenths, we have an example of diminution:

Augmentation is the opposite process, and usually it would be used to either slow down the overall movement of the piece or to create a dramatic and majestic effect:

Ornamentation is one of the oldest tools for improvisers and it is still one of the most effective.

Chapter 14

Modulation

This chapter introduces modulation and its use in improvisation.

Modulation is the process of moving the original melody and harmony up or down. Often the Dominant (V, G Major for C Major) relationship is used:

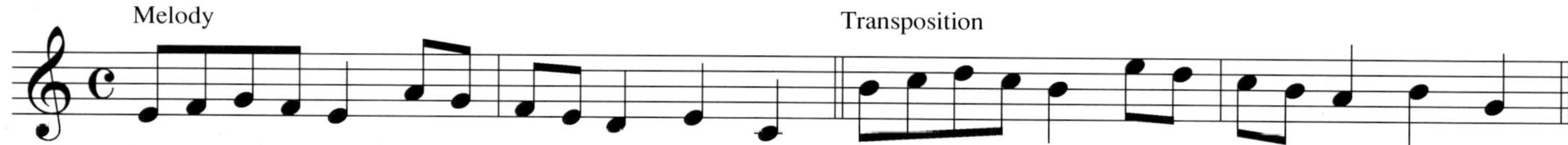

Another common relation is the subdominant (IV, F Major for C Major):

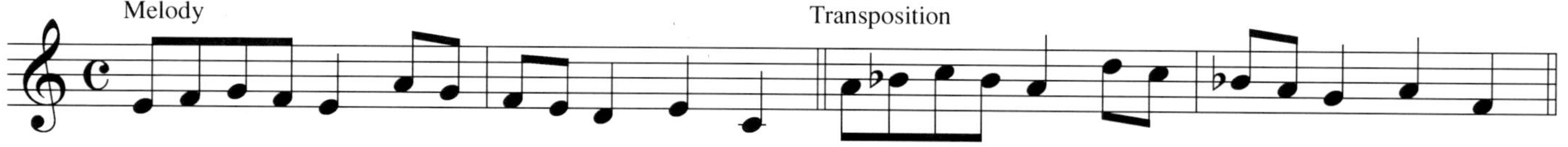

The harmonic tension of the Dominant towards the tonic is the strongest, and often when a subdominant modulation is used, it leads into the Dominant, which then goes to the tonic:

Sometimes only a couple of bars, usually of the beginning of the tune, are transposed while most of the original harmony stays intact. This is called fake modulation, and it can be used successfully for a temporary change of musical character in improvisation. In this case the variation begins with a clearly modulated statement but almost immediately goes back to the original melody:

Melody can also modulate a half step or a whole step up or down:

Modulation is a quite radical tool, and usually it is used after other forms of variation have been used already. For example, we could have an original melody, 4 variations in the original key, then a fake modulation to the subdominant key with an immediate return to the original key in variation 5, a modulation a whole step down in variation 6 and return to the tonic key with a slightly ornamented original melody.

Chapter Fifteen

Changing the Mode

This chapter introduces the change of mode as a way of varying the character of the melody.

One of the main characteristics of the melody is its mode. A very effective tool is to switch the mode to its opposite. The following example illustrates changing the Major mode of the melody to minor:

Just as well, minor melodies can be changed to Major, which sometimes leads to a triumphant feeling of victory:

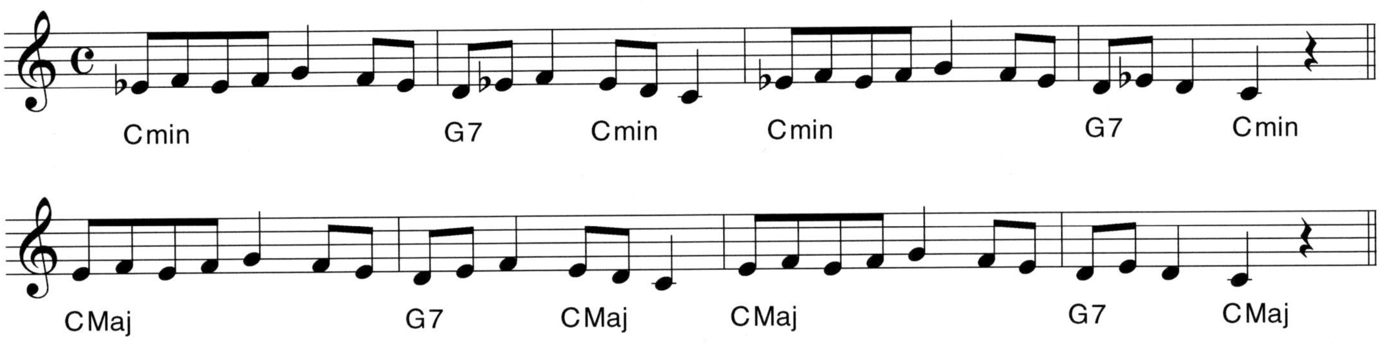

A more subtle change is using alternative forms of Major (Lydian, Mixolydian) and minor (dorian, phrygian):

Another possible change is using a diminished or augmented scale. However the character of these scales destroys any resemblance of the original harmony, therefore both of these scales are often used over long Dominant or subdominant pedal tones:

Change of mode is a very radical tool and needs to be used after many other variations have been used and the tonal character is well established. Usually the change of mode does not last long ending in a modulation to the original key.

Chapter Sixteen

Form

This chapter discusses overall form and planning of the form before starting the actual improvisation.

With the wide variety of tools we have already discovered, it is time now to speak about the complete improvised piece. Just as motivic development creates a melody out of a single motive, improvisation creates a whole piece of music. Usually the complete musical work can be looked upon as a philosophical statement. It begins with the statement of an idea. It then develops the idea resulting in a change of the original statement's character. At the end the opening statement returns similar to its original character.

This is the opening melody:

In Variation 1 the melody is varied only slightly:

Variation 2 develops the eighth note movement further using fewer elements of the original melody:

TRACK 36

Using diminution, variation 4 introduces triplets and sixteenth notes:

TRACK 37

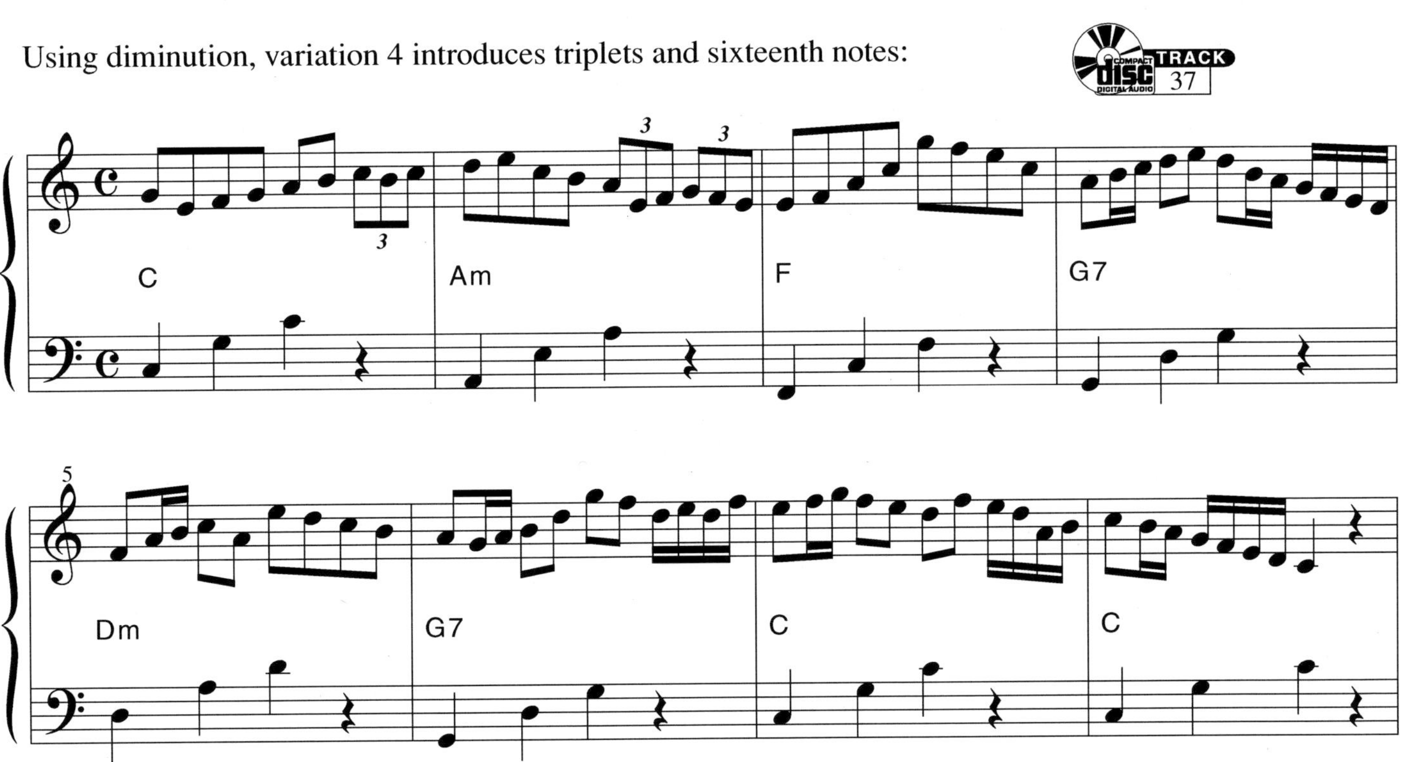

Variation 5 consists completely of sixteenth notes with very little resemblance to the original melody:

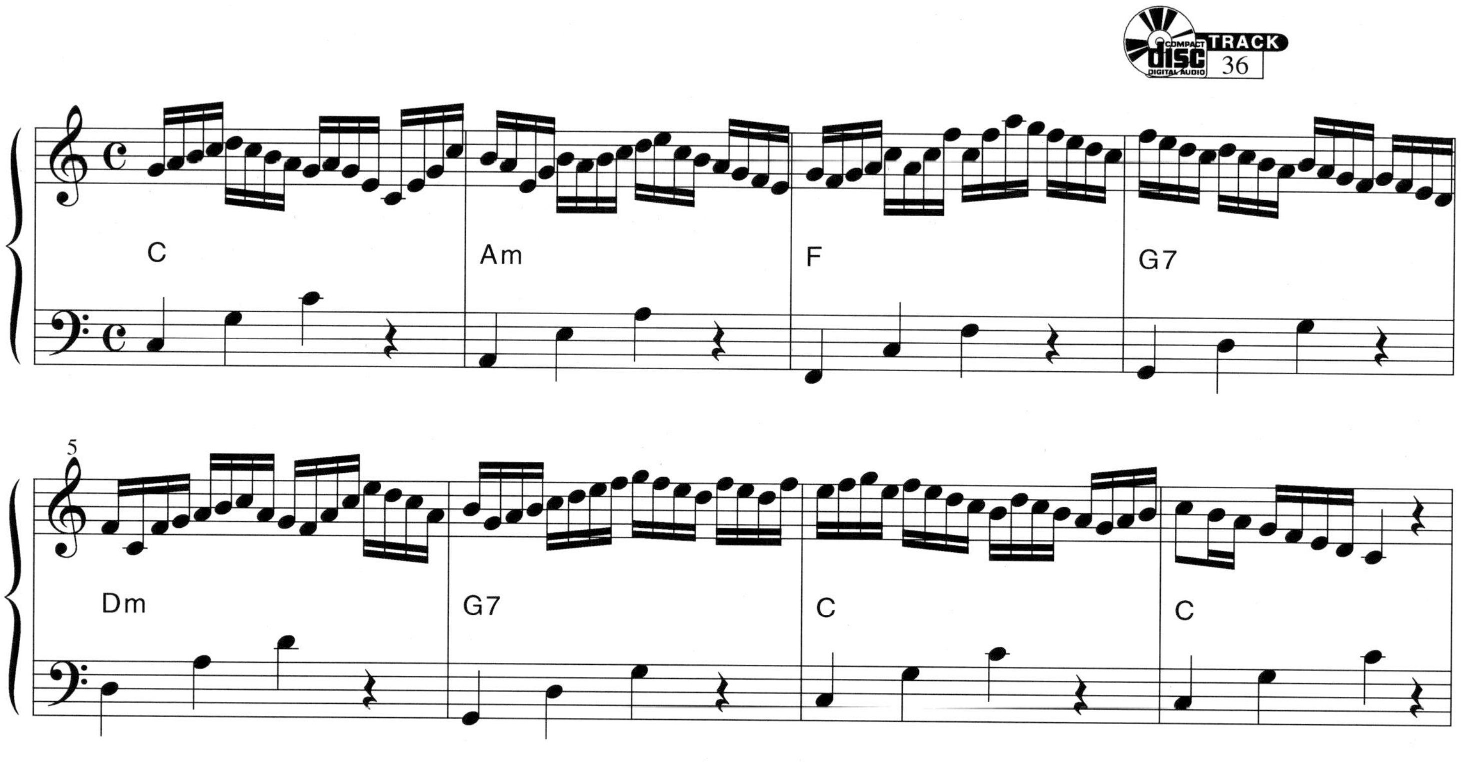

Variation 6 introduces a fake modulation of the original melody into Dominant key, quickly returning to the original key and continuing the sixteenth note movement:

Variation 7 brings the original melody in the minor mode. This is the greatest conflict of the piece:

Finally we have the return of the original melody in the original key. This completes the logical arch that holds the whole composition together:

Planning the whole piece is crucial to keep the listener interested and excited and to create a logically beautiful piece of music.

Chapter Seventeen

Range

This chapter discusses the use of the piano's range to improve dynamic development.

Another powerful tool to develop and suspend the interest of listeners is the efficient use of melodic range. Human psychology responds to melody as if it were sung by a human voice. For a singer, it is usually harder to sing high, and listeners respond to higher notes as more emotional and excited. The same response occurs in the case of the piano. The higher notes of the melody sound more emotional and less stable:

Thus the improvisation should be developed to slowly ascend to the higher note in the most dramatic part of the piece. A helpful analogy for melodic development is the concept of fighting gravity. The melodic line is trying to get up and conquer the mountain while gravity constantly tries to hold it down. Climbing up and reaching the high note, defying gravity, creates a sense of accomplishment, and returning home at the end creates a logical conclusion. The following example illustrates this idea using a short melodic segment:

This concept of piano range should be considered equally in planning motives, melodies and in the construction of the whole piece. In the following graph, range is displayed vertically and time horizontally:

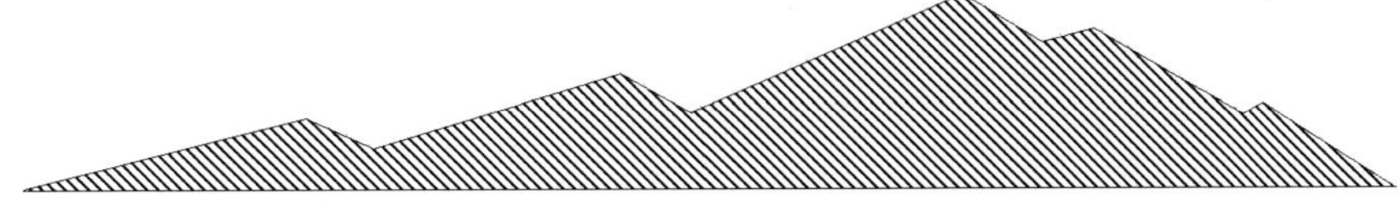

Chapter Eighteen

Left Hand Variations

This chapter introduces more advanced figures for the left hand.

Up to this point, we have used the same left hand variation for every example. In improvisation the accent is often put on the development of the right hand rather than the left. Improvising requires the creation of music on the spot, and the left hand often uses quite simple formulas to give the improviser more freedom for melodic development in the right hand. Nevertheless there is a variety of different formulas for the left hand which enhance the character of the different variations.

First we will introduce four slightly different left hand parts that can be used for improvisation:

The following example has four additional bass lines:

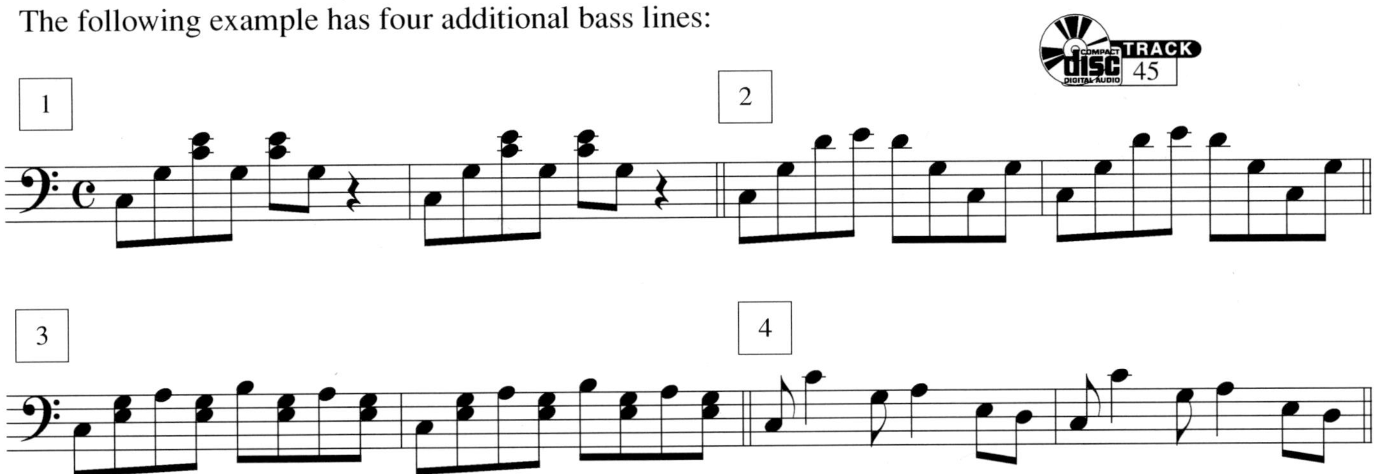

One of the most common left hand formulas in classical music is the Alberti bass. The following example has two variations of the Alberti bass:

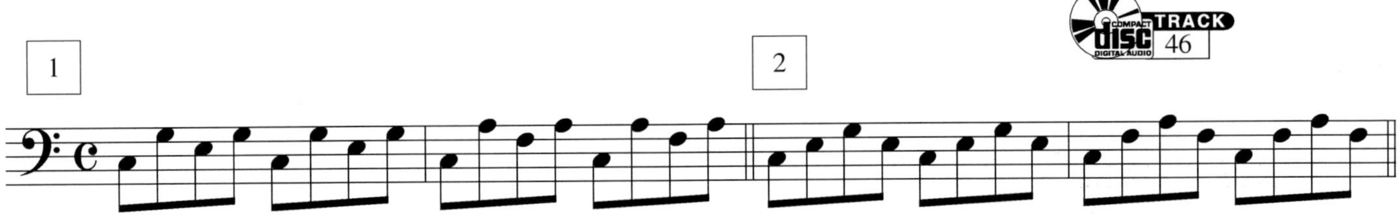

An important aspect in choosing the best left hand formula is the amount of movement it creates. Some bass lines slow the movement down and are more suitable for opening parts or possibly for contrasting slow variations in the middle:

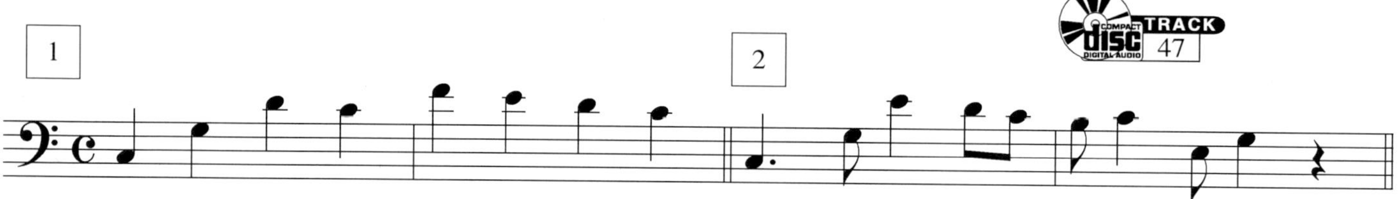

Other bass lines create more movement and are suitable for the main sections of fast variations in the middle of the piece:

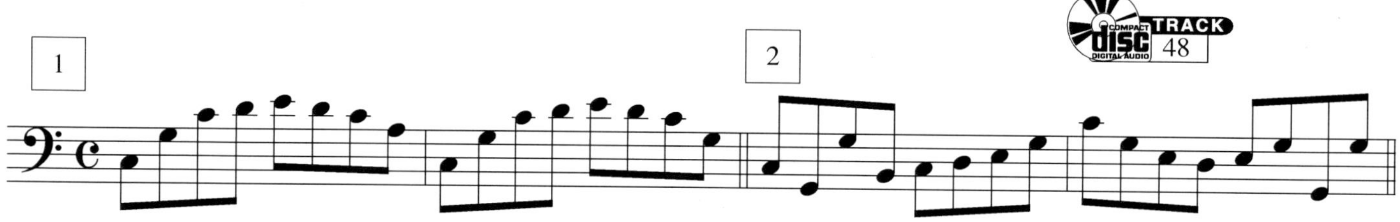

The following example illustrates the difference the left hand makes:

Overall, variations of the left hand in improvised music should be kept quite simple so as not to overpower the right hand.

Part III: Styles

Chapter Nineteen

Style: Introduction

This chapter introduces style and the four main types of music - March, Dance, Song and Free Form.

Style is developed as a result of improvising, composing and performing music in a particular historic period and in a particular geographic location. Different styles call for different types of harmony, accompaniment, ornamentation and other musical characteristics of the piece. To provide the basis for analyzing and improvising in any style, we will introduce some common styles and analyze them. There are four distinct types of music- song, march, dance and free form. Song is characterized by the attention given to the melody. March has a distinct walk-like, "marching" rhythm. Dance is also very rhythmical, but not as predictable and constant as march. Free form is usually introductory or intermediate music, often an instrumental prelude to a more substantial musical event.

Song melody should be very lyrical, and the accompaniment should merely support the melody and have no dominating character:

March is almost always written in 4/4 meter. The accompaniment is very sturdy, predictable, and usually quite loud. The main purpose of march is to provide a strong rhythmical structure for people marching:

Dance is in a way a combination of song and march. Both melody and rhythm are equally important:

Free form does not necessarily present strong melody or strong rhythm. Its purpose is to set up the mood for things to come:

Song, march, dance and free form can be traced to very early music, and they are still very recognizable in the music of today.

Chapter Twenty

March

This chapter introduces examples of different March styles.

Simple March is made up of a bass-chord left hand and a right hand that uses quarter notes, eighth notes and a dotted eighth-sixteenth combination:

The melodic structure should be kept very simple and repetitive. Originally march was meant for people to walk in time with, therefore it was loud and dynamically consistent:

Chords used in marches are full and have much doubling. The bass is often doubled by an octave; the right hand part can be treated similarly:

COMPACT disc DIGITAL AUDIO TRACK 57

March is a source for many different stylistic variations. The development of March incorporated more freedom of melody and rhythm, although the marching character of the music is still present:

COMPACT disc DIGITAL AUDIO TRACK 58

Some marches were written as fanfares- music for the opening of a ceremony. Usually these are written for trumpets and other brass instruments:

TRACK 59

Many marches were written for special, triumphant occasions and have a very grand and majestic character:

TRACK 60

A funeral march is quite the opposite. The two main characteristics of the funeral march are slow tempo and minor key:

Now, on the brighter side, one of the styles that developed with the march idea in mind is Ragtime, an all-American piano style:

Chapter Twenty-One

Dance Styles

This chapter introduces examples of different Dance styles.

Menuet is one of the earliest dance styles, written in 3/4 meter. It is a part of the baroque suite:

Waltz is a Romantic innovation. It often uses a very comfortable bass-chords formula in the left hand:

Mazurka is a Polish dance in ¾ meter, quite similar to waltz. The following example shows a melody from one of Chopin's mazurkas:

Polonaise is another Polish dance; here is another example from Chopin:

The last dance form we will mention is another American style called Boogie Woogie. It is the only form we discuss with a 12 bar form rather than 8 or 16 bar form. The left hand in Boogie Woogie uses a repeated figure based on the tonic of the chord:

TRACK 67

Here are some typical right hand formulas using triplets and repeated rhythmic chords called riffs. These formulas are used frequently in Boogie Woogie:

TRACK 68

Chapter Twenty-Two

Song Styles

This chapter introduces examples of different Song styles.

In Song styles, melody has a dominating character. The left hand can be very simple. In fact, the very first left hand we introduced in chapter one would be quite typical:

Sometimes the simple dance left hand is used, but it should be played more softly and lyrically than in a dance piece:

Nocturne literally means night-time, and it is a lyrical piece with a subtle, quiet character and a very developed melody:

On the other hand, song can use a strict dance accompaniment, incorporating a dance-like character:

The last example of song we will analyze is a popular song, which uses a repetitive pattern in the left hand. The right hand plays a melody supported by chords:

The most important aspect of improvising in song styles is to keep the melody as the dominating part over the accompaniment.

Chapter Twenty-Three

Free-Form Styles

This chapter introduces examples of different Free-form styles.

We will start with a Prelude imitating the strumming of a guitar:

TRACK 74

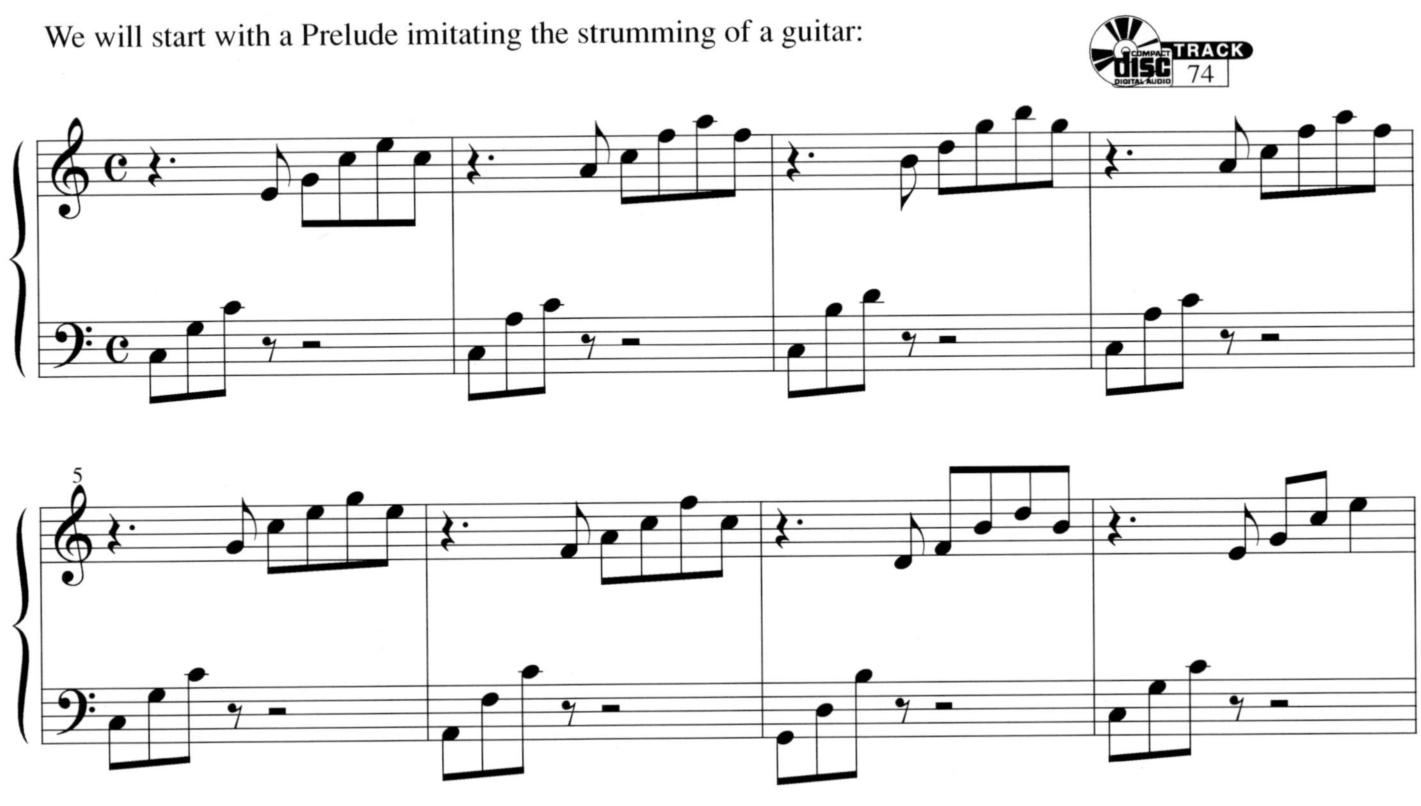

The use of this material in keyboard music leads to many wonderful compositions like the next example- one of Bach's preludes:

TRACK 75

The same idea resulted in this piece also written by Bach:

Another source of inspiration for free-form improvisation is Italian recitative:

Using long sustained chords is a very effective tool to generate tension. Free-forms are great for introducing a piece with a more distinct character.

Chapter Twenty-Four

Stylistic Modulation

This chapter introduces modulation from one style to another while improvising.

Just as we can use modulation into new key or change of the mode, we can change the style of the variation. The following example consists of a four-bar phrase in two completely different styles, yet they can follow each other as variations on the same melody:

Sometimes the stylistic change can be very subtle without causing any big dramatic events:

The style change can also be very dramatic. In this case, it should only be used in the appropriate part of the form, before the return of the original melody:

An interesting effect is changing the meter of the original melody; this usually causes a stylistic change as well:

A stylistic change can also be used for the last exposition of the melody to improve its effectiveness or change its character.

Chapter Twenty-Five

Using Foreign Material

This chapter discusses introducing foreign material into the piece.

Sometimes it is possible to use completely new material in the middle of variations. The most known example of the use of foreign material in classical music is the introduction of the Ode to Joy in Beethoven's 9th Symphony. Philosophically, the new material often contradicts the main melody:

Although this is a rather free way of creating musical material, there are certain rules which apply to the use of foreign material:

1. It should be quite impressive by itself.
2. It should contrast the previous material.
3. It should be very recognizable
4. It should make some elegant logical construction with the rest of the piece.

In other words, it has to make sense. It should never be a random piece of music that unpredictably breaks the development of musical material without purpose.

We are now familiar with the alphabet and language of improvisation in some of the classical styles. Improvising can only be learned and developed by practice. It is also very important to set clear goals in every improvisation. Think of the form and the musical language before starting to play. It will help to avoid the occurrence of repetition instead of true improvisation.

Improvisation is a very rewarding process. The pianist becomes a creator of music, and best of all, the results are achieved immediately. Improvisation is a great tool to experiment with different sounds, ideas and concepts. Most great musicians of the past were able to improvise very well, and the ability to improvise is also very valuable today. Improvisation gives musicians deep understanding of musical material and their role in creating it.

Variations on a Theme by Beethoven from Piano Sonata, Op. 57

Misha V. Stefanuk

Theme

mf

4

7

10

f

13
mf
Variation 1
TRACK
84
Eighth note movement in the right hand is supported by the left hand from the Theme
16
f
mp
19
22
25
f

28
mf
Variation 2
TRACK
85
Eighth notes are combined with triplets and sixteenths
31
f
mf
34
37
40
mp

43
p
46
Variation 3
TRACK
86
Further development of eighths, triplets and sixteenths with less resemblance to the main Theme
49
mp
52
54

57
59
61
f
mp
Variation 4
COMPACT disc DIGITAL AUDIO
TRACK 87
Sixteenth note movement takes over the entire musical material
64
mf
66

68
mf
70
72
mf
74
76
f
mf

78
Variation 5
TRACK
88
81 False modulation into Dominant with a fast return to the original key
mf
84
3
87
f
89
mf

91
93
Variation 6
TRACK
89
Changing the Mode of the Theme
95
98
101

104
mp
107
mf
mf
110
Return of the Theme
TRACK
90
Slightly modified version with a Dominant pedal and a more exciting cadence
112
f
f
115
f
mf

118
121
mp
mf
124
mf
mp
mf
127
mf
rit.
f

About the Author

Mel Bay best-selling author, Misha V. Stefanuk, started playing piano at the age of five. He composed his first piece when he was nine. Mr. Stefanuk graduated from Boston University (M.M. in Music Education), Belmont University (B.M. in Music Composition) and Moscow Conservatory School (B.M. in Music Theory). Misha also studied at Moscow Studio of Music Improvisation Art, the Russian Academy of Music, where Misha was a student of Kirill Volkov, Aram Khachaturian's assistant and Dmitry Blum, Skidmore Jazz Institute, and Washington State University, studying with Gregg Yasinitsky, Charles Argersinger and Frank Mantooth. Misha has written more then 120 works for a variety of instrumentations, as well as music for over thirty theater shows, including an original score for Y2K Survival Guide with Leonard Nemoy. Misha has composed a significant amount of music for network television, including programs such as All My Children and One Life to Live (ABC), Passions (NBC), The Chris Isaak Show (Showtime) Young and the Restless and First Monday (CBS). Among his works are the Mel Bay best-sellers Jazz Piano Chords (nr.1 in Jazz Piano since 2002), Jazz Piano Scales (nr.3 since 2004) and Jazz Piano for the Young Beginner (nr.2 since 2005), Jazz Piano Album (2005) and Piano for Adults (2003).

Mr. Stefanuk is a monthly columnist for Creative Keyboard and a regular judge at the Chopin Youth Piano Competition in Milwaukee, Wisconsin. Mr. Stefanuk is a prize-winner of the Stereotypes and Nations Composition Competition held by Muzica Centrum Art Society in Cracow, Poland for his composition Equinokse for oboe, string trio and prepared piano, and of the Concerto Aria Composition Competition at Belmont University for his piece The New American Symphony. He was also named Outstanding Piano Player at the l29th Annual Lionel Hampton Jazz Festival, and has won full scholarships at Belmont University, Washington State University, and Skidmore Summer Jazz Institute.
Misha and his wife, Evan, teach over one hundred students at Johnson Ferry Conservatory of Music in Atlanta Georgia and privately. Among them are recording artists, TV personalities, winners of national and regional competitions, and teachers. Misha's students attended a number of prestigious music schools in US, and abroad. Mr. Stefanuk has released over twenty CDs varying from Contemporary Classical to Jazz, New Age and Pop, including a recording of Bach's Inventions.

Visit Misha's web sites at www.stefanuk.com, www.stefanukmusic.com and www.thenewopera.com

EXCELLENCE IN MUSIC
MEL BAY®
Since 1947